LIBERTARIAN ECONOMICS: A MANIFESTO AND AN EXPLANATION

Russell Hasan

CONTENTS

LIBERTARIAN ECONOMICS: A MANIFESTO

This paper will use the following abbreviated notations:

L&E: law and economics.

C/C: the approach based on Coase and Calabresi.

Max EE: the goal, or condition, of maximizing economic efficiency. Specifically, a maximum amount of money made (AMM) net sum of all economic actors in a scenario.

L&E1: the view of L&E that the goal of L&E is to internalize negative and/or positive externalities by simulating zero transaction costs. Law and Economics version 1.0.

L&E2: the view of L&E that the goal of L&E is Max EE. Also known as Law and Economics version 2.0.

P: a Polluter.

R: a Resident.

R1: a first radio station.

R2: a second radio station.

C: Cost.

AMM: Amount of Money Made.

PAMM: Potential Amount of Money Made (AMM plus opportunity cost).

The OPIE Principle: Output = Process of Input Plus Error. In economic terms, the input is the Cost, and the output is the Benefit. If Benefit exceeds Cost, the difference is the Profit. If Cost exceeds Benefit, the difference is the Loss. Cost and Benefit are precisely mathematically defined by a given Process.

The $1 Principle: If economic rational self-interest is conceded, then, to the same extent that a $10,000 profit is better than a $250 profit, it is equally true that a $10,001 profit is better than a $10,000 profit. If you can get an extra dollar of Benefit for an equal or lesser Cost then there is no rational reason not to do so.

The Opportunity Cost Principle: If X makes $500 and Y makes $100 and you can do X or Y but not both, then not doing Y is the Opportunity Cost of doing X, which means that, to sum all Benefits and Costs for X, you must also include a $100 loss from not having done Y. The Opportunity Cost is real, not merely theoretical, because, had you done Y instead of X, then the $100 would have been real, not mere abstract theory.

Let us begin with Coase Theorem.[1] Assume that P (Polluter) has $1 million AMM (Amount of Money he Makes) if he pollutes, and further assume that his pollution is toxic pollution which will seep into the property of R (Resident) and this will make

R too sick to work. Assume R's AMM is $30,000 from his day job as a laborer. Assume that if R sues and blocks P from polluting then the $1 million AMM is lost. Assume that if R gets sick from toxic pollution his $30,000 AMM is destroyed. Posit a goal of Max EE defined such that the sum of AMM of all economic actors is maximized.

So we can summarize the scenario as:

R: $30,000.

P: $1,000,000.

R Minus P = -$970,000 (R = +$30,000 and P = $-1,000,000).

P Minus R = $970,000 (P = +$1,000,000 and R = $-30,000).

If R sues and blocks the polluting conduct of P then $1 million is lost but $30,000 is gained, a net loss of $970,000. Therefore let P pollute is the Max EE result. But then R dies (although, in most of the cases of this example in the literature, it is noise pollution, so R just loses $30,000 worth of the quiet enjoyment of his estate.) How do we solve this problem so R lives while P is free and Max EE is achieved?

Coase Theorem became famous as an innovative solution: Let P pay R an amount in excess of R's loss so that R will consent to P's pollution, freely and without coercion.

If P pays R $60,000 to let P pollute, P's after the fact AMM is $940,000, R gets sick and loses $30,000 but gains $60,000 so his net AMM is $30,000, and the sum of AMM of R and P is $970,000, which represents a swing of $970,000 compared to R blocking P.

Let's Summarize this as:

P: $1,000,000.

R: $30,000.

P minus R = $970,000.

P Gives $60,000 to R.

Now P = $940,000 ($1,000,000 - $60,000) and R = $30,000 (-$30,000 + $60,000). So the net sum of all parties is still $970,000, but P has freedom and both P and R have made a profit.

Here we reach some conclusions of Coase Theorem: let P pay R to pollute, and unless blocking P nets over the $1 million cost of blocking P and have some profit on top of it then don't block P. So let P pay R in this hypo, but if, to change the fact pattern, R is an entrepreneur who makes $1,200,000, then R should block P, because $1 million is lost but $1.2 million is saved so there is a net profit of $200,000 as the net sum of AMM of all economic actors. All entirely by reference only to Max EE.

Guido Calabresi is widely viewed as having achieved the one great innovative improvement upon Coase's original work. His theory became known as "Rule 4."

We can arrive at Calabresi and the "Rule 4" theory that he famously articulated in this way.[2] Rule 4 posits that, instead of P paying R to bear pollution, if R can force P not to pollute (in an environmentalist utopia) then P should be able to force R to pay to P the cost of not polluting. P should be allowed to pollute unless R can pay P his cost not to pollute, then if we let P force R to pay him not to pollute, either R can and does (if the benefit to R exceeds $1 million then this results in Max EE) or if he does not and cannot (and on the previous numbers he can't afford to because his benefit is $30,000) then P should pollute and Max EE is achieved, and the benefit to R is destroyed, and AMM equals $1 million minus R's lost AMM. R's benefit must exceed $1 million for him to pay P because P could only be paid the cost of not polluting if the payment equals or exceeds P's lost AMM, which is $1 million.

Diagram this as:

P = $1,000,000.

If $R > $P, R pays R – P to P and keeps the difference.

If $P > $R, P makes $1,000,000 and either P keeps 100% and R suffers a loss of $R or else P keeps $P – $R and P gives $R to R.

Assume R and P in a Rule 4 world, where P could pollute a little bit less and lose $30,000 and R would then not get sick. In this scenario the Cost of $30,000 of P's AMM is $30,000 of Cost to R, meaning R loses $30,000 for P to make a marginal additional $30,000, therefore the net sum of AMM remains the same whether P pollutes or R forces P not to pollute and R keeps his wages or R forces P not to pollute but P forces R to pay P what it is worth to not pollute. A $30,000 gain to P is a $30,000 loss to R, and vice versa, so the net sum of all parties is constant.

If R keeps his wages, R makes $30,000 and P makes $970,000 and the sum of AMM of all parties is $1 million. If P forces R to pay him $30,000 to pollute less, R pays $30,000 but gains $30,000, and P makes $970,000 and gets paid $30,000, hence nets $1 million, or at P's discretion he chooses full pollution and makes $1 million. Rule 4 is proven because in terms of AMM the results are identical if P has freedom to pollute or force R to pay P his cost of not polluting if R forces P not to pollute.

We can diagram this as:

R forces P to pollute less and R doesn't get sick:

P $1,000,000 – P $30,000 (the cost of polluting less) + R $30,000 (now R doesn't get sick, hence R's income) = $1,000,000.

Or:

P forces R to pay P the value, to R, of P polluting less:

P $1,000,000 – P $30,000 = P $970,000 + R $30,000 (R's income) – R $30,000 (R loses what he pays to P) + $30,000 for P (what R pays to P) = $1,000,000.

In contrast, if P fully pollutes, P = $1,000,000 + P $30,000 (what P avoids losing) – R $30,000 (what R now loses) = $1,000,000.

So the Calabresi Rule 4 Conclusion is that, in this scenario, it doesn't make any difference, to P or to us, whether P fully pollutes, or is forced by R not to pollute, because, as weird as this sounds, if R can force P not to pollute and achieve a Max EE result then P could force R to force P not to pollute and achieve the same Max EE result, that is, if R forces P to pay R the cost of the negative externality of P's pollution, this achieves a result identical to P forcing R to pay P the negative impact, upon P, that R has on P by forcing upon P the internalizing of the negative externality that P forced onto R. Basically, it all sums net to the same result, because the Benefits and Costs are the same.

The only question is how those Benefits and Costs are distributed, whether R gets them or P gets them, which is a political question, not an economic question, as will be discussed below. For the economy, the only thing that the economy wants is Max EE, because Max EE is maximum profit, maximum Benefit over Cost net sum of all parties, and that maximizes the wealth that humanity has to spend for the survival of the human species.

However, let us now turn to the question of distribution. You might assume that distribution is defined by the initial distribution of rights: If R has the right to block P's pollution, then P will be forced to pay R. But if P has the initial right to pollute, then P won't give R any money. But Coase Theorem says no, that is not really true, we end up with the same result regardless of initial distribution. Why?

This paper goes "back to formula" by examining the Radio Station Scenario, which was the first hypothetical Coase analyzed before he turned his attention to the more popular Pollution Nuisance Scenario.

Let us next consider two radio stations where

the federal regulators must choose one and only one to assign a license for a radio spectrum (essentially a license to operate) to.[3] Assume radio stations named R1 and R2. R1 has a bigger market and a better product than R2. R1 has a PAMM (Potential Amount of Money it will Make if licensed) of $90,000. R2 has a PAMM of $30,000 if licensed.

If R1 gets the license, R2 goes out of business, net AMM is $60,000 ($90,000 of R1 minus lost R2 $30,000). If R2 gets the license and the license is alienable, R1 can buy the license from R2 for $30,001. R2 still goes out of business and loses $30,000 PAMM but gets paid $30,001 so is $1 better off and R1 nets $59,999 AMM ($90,000 in AMM minus the $30,001 payment). So $60,000 in AMM results either way, because this is equal to R1's AMM ($59,999) plus R2's AMM ($30,001) minus R2's loss of PAMM ($30,000), proving the Coase Theorem that it doesn't matter who gets the license in a free economy because the Max EE result will happen either way.

We can diagram this as:

R1: PAMM $90,000.

R2: PAMM $30,000.

R1 – R2 = $60,000.

R2 – R1 = $-60,000. (R2 – R1 = $30,000 – $90,000).

Or:

If R2 gets the license and then R1 buys the license from R2:

R1: +$90,000 -$30,001. Net plus $59,999.

R2: -$30,000 +$30,001. Net plus $1.

R1: $59,999 (final).

R2: $30,001 (final).

AMM net sum of all parties: $60,000 ($59,999 + $1) (Max EE).

The central thesis of L&E2 is that, if zero transaction costs exist, the initial distribution of rights and decision-making authority does not matter. R1 or R2 may have the license. P or R may decide who is forced to pay. It does not matter. The maximum economically efficient outcome will naturally arise from any scenario, because it will either exist initially or it will pay for itself to arise and come into being if it did not exist initially. By having the most AMM, the Max EE outcome can outbid any alternative and is therefore a logically necessary outcome as a result of free market capitalism. It is inevitable.

The key takeaway from this is that the initial distribution of rights does not matter, because, if the economy is perfectly free (with zero transaction costs), then the Max EE result will naturally be the end-result, no matter what. Whether Radio Station One or Radio Station Two is given the license initially, the one that makes the most profit will emerge as the owner and victor, although the other one still ends up being better off than in any alternative possibility. Max EE is the "pareto-optimal" condition, to use an academic phrasing, which means that no one could be made better off by any changes.

To paraphrase F.A. Hayek, this means that order will naturally emerge from chaos, automatically, because the economics will cause it to happen, regardless of which chaotic scenario is the starting point. By analogy, this applies to the Liberty Movement: given any starting distribution of power, whether power is given to kings and emperors and dictators, or feudal lords, or to corrupt Liberal or Conservative politicians, or to the public democratically, the Liberty Movement will win, eventually, and Libertarianism will be the end result, one the wars and conflicts of politics sort themselves out and resolve, into a historically predetermined and inevitable conclusion, because Liberty is the Max EE political and economic system.

We are at a moment in history when the Liberty Movement has just begun, when there are still people alive today who met Ayn Rand and Murray Rothbard in person, but, given enough passage of time, and future generations, we can foretell how history will unfold.

Law and Economics dovetails with Public Choice Theory, the school of thought which examines the motivations of politicians in the most cynical lens possible and assumes that each politician just acts to maximize their own self-interest, and never purely for the good of society, in this way: if government and politicians try to block the Max EE outcome, the Max EE outcome will simply bribe them or pay to create a structure where their self-interest aligns with itself, because the maximum profit will result if and to the extent that the money made from doing so exceeds the costs, so the money spent will pay for itself. Government can only prevail when its control is so oppressive that the costs of circumventing it exceed the profits in the condition of economic freedom.

For example, assume R and P, P has AMM of $1 million, R has AMM of $30,000. Assume an environmentalist lobbying group and a politician who favors them. Assume P can buy the politician with a $200,000 campaign contribution, can sway the lobby by donating $100,000 to fund clean energy research, and faces at worst a $500,000 fine if accused of bribery and corruption. The AMM is $1 million and the Cost is $830,000, so the pollution will happen, regardless of whether P or the politician holds the initial decision-making power.

So we can diagram this as:

P: $1,000,000.

R: $30,000.

Bribe the political system (Liberals, L): $800,000.

Because P > R + L, P is the Max EE Result, so P will happen, and P will keep $P – $L as a profit, and $R is just a negative externality loss that R suffers.

You might think that the Libertarian would just let the pollution happen, and let P keep the full amount of $P, while the Liberal would want P to pay the corruption and bribery fee to the political system to let the pollution happen. However, if R has an individual right, such as ownership of body (health) or property (land) which P's pollution would violate, then P would have to pay R, because R could block the pollution as of legal right, because moral natural rights are prior to economic efficiency according to Libertarian political values. Thus, the key Coase Theorem insight that you would pay people an amount equal to their cost of your benefit holds true.

From the economy's point of view, it makes no difference to society whether the profit is distributed to P or to the Liberal politicians, because Max EE is achieved regardless, so long as the pollution happens. P will make $P, and R will be paid according to R's role in the profit-making, to the extent that P must internalize negative externalities.

Only the Marxist socialist would completely block the pollution. Here we reach a point in our analysis where we Libertarians can gleefully prove that the Marxist socialist will never overcome the resistance of moderate Liberals among the Left: If the cost of funding a political system for the Liberals to usurp and control the Marxist socialists, thereby allowing business to make a profit, is less than the value of capitalism to the rich businesspeople, then big business will simply pay for a corrupt Liberal political system that will not allow the Marxist socialists to ever completely block business or to block the pollution of a P on behalf of an R.

In any society with the rule of law and which lacks a Marxist socialist dictatorship, if a rich business party to a lawsuit can afford far better lawyers than a poor individual party, and the profit to be made from winning the litigation exceeds the cost of the lawyers for the business, then the maximally efficient result is for the business to do the objectionable conduct, hire the lawyers and win and pay the legal fees, which are the cost of winning. And of course the lawyers and the judge both went to Harvard Law School where they were friends and frat brothers and went to the same parties and were at each others' weddings and all it takes is a wink and a nudge from the law firm, and P wins the case, and poor R with his local small law firm attorney never had a prayer. This is the corruption of Liberal economics, which only Libertarian economics can overcome.

If a business can make $1 million from pollution, and win an environmentalist lawsuit by paying $750,000 of legal fees, then it has to pollute. Economic rational self-interest dictates this. Much as we might feel this is repulsive, or unethical, basic economics and math defines this as the necessary and logical result.

Business breaking law (Benefit): $1,000,000.
Legal fees of breaking the law (Cost): $750,000.
Profit: $250,000.

Going back to the $1 Principle, even if Liberals impose a high Cost of doing business in a regulated Liberal economy, the rich businesspeople will pay it, because they benefit more by paying it and making the money than by not doing business at all (being blocked). The Liberals don't want to stop Capitalism, they just want to redistribute its results, to the poor (so they say) or, for the corrupt Liberal politicians, into their own pockets on behalf of their poor voters. It is only the Marxist socialists who truly want to destroy Capitalism, in the interests of their pure ideals, but the purity of their ideals collapse to the extent that economics is rational and a necessary and ethical component of human existence for life on earth.

And, much as their ideals seem pure but are really not, so, too, all Marxist socialism will inevitably disintegrate into Liberal corruption, that, as a Liberal politician just wants a bribe or a fine to be paid, the Marxist socialist dictator who enslaves an economy will end up using corruption to line his own pockets at the expense of his people. It is inevitable, and is what the science of economics would predict and expect.

Assume the following scenarios:

P is a public company, R is a shareholder, C is the cost of paying a fine to the SEC for breaking an SEC rule. If the value to P of breaking the law exceeds C, then P will break the law and pay the fine to the SEC. If the benefit to the SEC of collecting the fine exceeds the benefit to the SEC of enforcing the law, then the SEC would rather have P break the law and pay the fine than have P obey the law. In this way, the existence of the rules and regulations creates a system whereby people find it in their economic self-interest to be corrupt and to promote corruption. Regulations lead inevitably to institutionalized bribery.

A Liberal political system, where the Liberals say that greed is evil, and pass laws and regulations to prevent big business from doing business and making money, but which laws the businesspeople must break to make the money that pays for humanity to survive, and then must pay fines to the Liberal government as the cost of doing business, constitutes little more than a "protection racket," much as the mafia or organized crime frequently runs. The Liberals "protect" business and "protect" the free market, and "protect" the public from the free market, and let business be free, in return for taking a bribe, collecting fines and legal fees and lobbying donations, skimming something off the top, taking a haircut.

The Liberals say they hate business and greed, but their only desire is to take as much money from the rich for themselves as possible, which is both hypocrisy and corruption. The true Liberal secretly loves Capitalism because Capitalism maximizes the amount of wealth available for them to steal. I will concede that, if Capitalism exists, the PAMM is roughly constant between Liberty and Liberalism, the only difference between Liberty and Liberalism is that they both allow Capitalism but the Liberals distribute the proceeds and profits into corrupt politics, while Liberty lets everyone be free to own the rewards of their own hard work, so you keep your own profit. Liberalism holds business hostage, and demands as ransom that business pays taxes and pays the fines and penalties of disobeying regulations. The Liberty Movement will set business free.

As such, Liberty is better than Liberalism because it is more ethical, and so is favorable to all humans in our capacity as moral agents. From the point of view of economic efficiency, Liberty says that pure free market economics actually makes more money than Liberalism, because getting the bad laws and rules out of the way makes more business and more profit possible, but the Liberal counter is that, from a Max EE point of view, Liberty and Liberalism are identical, because the Liberal never expects Capitalism to actually obey the rules, they expect the rich and big business to break the rules and then pay the fines, which fines the Liberal politicians and activists happily collect and pocket for themselves.

Only by means of Libertarianism, where there are no laws or fines, would it be in everyone's self-interest to be ethical and honorable. And, in a Liberty Utopia, R does not need the Liberals to protect R from P, because R can protect themselves from P by means of private lawsuits, and thereby force P to internalize any negative externalities for R. If R enforces R's moral natural rights by private lawsuit, not by regulation and taxation and redistribution, then P is forced to pay R the cost of P's conduct, assuming that R can prove damages and culpability of P to a jury and judge. It is textbook

Libertarian law that every human has the right to own body (health) and property (land, possessions), so the rich could not trample these rights at will, and must pay to buy consent in a Liberty Utopia.

For example, if a public company stock commits a fraud upon an investor, in Liberalism, R relies on the SEC and its regulations to protect R, but P can just pay a fine to the SEC and walk away. In a Liberty Utopia, R would sue P directly, asserting fraud as a violation of moral natural rights to property embodied by contract law, and thereby R has control, and R can force P to compensate R and pay the cost of P's evil conduct. This is why both the rich Conservatives and the rich Liberals hate Libertarians and the Liberty Movement, because we would actually enable poor R to hold rich P accountable, in a way that does not currently happen in the corrupt Liberal-Conservative status quo.

It might be objected that P will just hire better lawyers than R, and so get away with murder, much as I described above. If the profit to be made from bribing judges and bribing the legal system exceeds the cost, then P will try to do so. But, I answer that, in a Liberty Utopia, we have gotten rid of all the hypocrisy and corruption, so that the judges and the legal system will have moral integrity and consistency and coherence. With just, simple, basic laws, laws written and intended for people to be able to obey while living happy lives, and not laws "made to be broken," it should be pretty obvious whether

R deserves to win or lose according to the letter of the law, and we can assume judges who will act with integrity, honor, and justice, which it would be impossible to bribe by hiring rich fancy lawyers or handing bribe money under-the-table.

No system is perfect, but Libertarian laws, and Libertarian justice, would be upheld in a Liberty Utopia, and it should be illegal for P to violate R's right to life, liberty and property, absent R's consent, in such a system, even if P is rich and R is poor and it is Max EE for P to do so. In that narrow scenario, P will just pay R a sum to buy R's consent, and R will make a profit on selling whatever permissions P wants, which, if R is poor and P is rich, could let R make far more money than R otherwise would.

Here is where a Liberty Utopia diverges from the Conservative L&E fantasy, because the Conservatives would like the rich to be able to do whatever they want, including violate the rights of the poor and the middle class, at will, just because it might be the Max EE result for those with more money to always win. In contrast, in a Liberty Utopia, there are Libertarian laws, and both rich, poor, and middle class, are equally held to obey those laws, without any corruption or hypocrisy.

In a Liberty Utopia, if rich P wants to steal from poor R, and it is actual theft of R's life, liberty or property, that R legitimately owns, then P cannot. And, in a Liberty Utopia, there is no fine nor bribe that P can pay to be able to do so, unlike in the Liberal-Conservative nightmare, because either P pays R a sum that R consents to for the release of R's right, or else P is blocked, by a judge and police when R sues P and wins.

But, in a Liberty Utopia, with zero transaction costs, P has the freedom to negotiate and bargain with R and pay R for R's consent to what P wants, making both R and P better off than they otherwise would be, whereas the Marxist socialist just blocks P from doing anything, as of right, without recourse, and thereby leaves no free path along which business can operate.

Assume the point of view that a capitalist economy PAMM will make $20 trillion GDP (this is roughly the amount of US GDP in 2020, source: Google and Wikipedia), but that, if it is unregulated "cowboy" free market capitalism, then the working class will rise up in Marxist socialist revolution and destroy it. Assume further that the PAMM of the same nation in a Marxist socialist economic system is $2 trillion, because they block lots of things that businesspeople need to do in order to make money, with regulations and red tape and just flat out not letting businesses operate because they hate greed and they hate money.

Assume that the rich capitalist businesspeople believe that, if they pay 20% of capital gains tax and corporate income tax to the government, that would be $4 trillion in taxes, which could fund a government Liberal welfare state, and that, if a Liberal welfare state exists, there won't be enough angry poor people to start a revolution. Then the welfare state becomes a cost of capitalism and of making a profit, which, if the rich feel the benefit exceeds the cost, then they make a profit, and will happily pay the tax, indeed their economic self-interest dictates they must, and must want to, pay taxes, because they maximize profit more in capitalism than in Marxist socialism.

In this way, the capitalist economy will motivate a Liberal movement where the Left will be trying to distribute as much for the working class as they can get, by means of enabling and conceding to a corrupt system. The only alternatives to this, are two systems, which have ethical integrity and honor, and those would be Marxist socialism, which can't exist because the rich will pay the political fees to prevent it from happening, or Libertarian Anarcho-Capitalism, where everyone will be perfectly free so there will be no occasion to pay bribery and corruption costs to the political system.

So we can diagram this hypothetical fact-pattern as:

Capitalism: $20 trillion.

Marxist socialism: $2 trillion.

Capitalism – Marxist Socialism = $20 trillion – $2 trillion = $18 trillion.

Then Capitalism could spend up to $18 trillion minus $1 in order to defeat Marxist socialism and still make a profit on the transaction.

The only question then becomes, from Capitalism's view, how to spend that $18 trillion?

The Liberal answer is: pay it to the government for the welfare state, which means, bribe the politicians with money, and bribe the working class with entitlements, to get the Liberals to allow Capitalism to exist. Such as, for example, a $4 trillion welfare state. $4 trillion means nothing to rich people who would own $16 trillion, it is crumbs to them.

The Libertarian answer, in contrast, is: spend that money on business, and reinvest it into capitalist free enterprise, which really means, let each person keep, and own, the money they make, instead of stealing some or all of that money as taxes for Liberal politicians to distribute to their voters. This is more honest and therefore less corrupt.

The Liberals and Conservatives both seem to concede that some of that money should be taxed and spent to bribe the working class into allowing Capitalism to exist, they just fight over exactly how much, with the Liberals wanting a little more for the poor, and the Conservatives wanting a little more for the rich. But they fight over distribution, not over the principle of corruption. Only the Liberty movement has an alternative to corruption as the cost of Capitalism. That alternative's name is: freedom.

Capitalism is going to exist. So why not let it exist? Why not let it be free? We do not need the welfare state to bribe the Left and the working class into allowing freedom to exist. You can never achieve victory for freedom by conceding to the State that the State has the right to destroy freedom.

The Liberty movement is all about principles, not making compromises with corruption, not forcing life to bribe death for the right to be alive. The more money you pay to death, the shorter your life will become. Freedom, to be truly free, must be legalized, with no taxes and no regulations, and, if a Marxist socialist revolution rises up, you could spend up to $18 trillion to put it down. But, with a democracy, we decide things by votes, not by revolutions, so the Liberty movement can win, even without any bloodshed.

If AMM of Capitalism = $20 trillion, then, from society's point of view, it doesn't make any difference what portion of that is kept by the rich business world or is distributed to the poor welfare state, provided that, assuming that AMM of Capitalism = $20 trillion and AMM of Marxist Socialism = $2 trillion, the system will do anything possible to keep capitalism and avoid socialism to thereby prevent society and the human species from suffering a $28 trillion loss. So Left vs. Right, Liberals vs. Conservatives, is just a fight over whether the AMM of their corrupt political system of corruption is distributed to the rich or distributed to the poor, they have no self-interested motivation in reform or honor or ethical integrity.

Ayn Rand made a clever and insightful argument: the Liberals and Conservatives concede Capitalism as the means of production, but then they fight over distribution. But this is like saying that we must have theft and stealing from a business so that we will let the businessperson work without us putting our foot on their neck and kicking them in the face. This is like saying that business is a necessary evil, which we will tolerate so long as they pay money to the welfare state, so the poor and the working class don't revolt. But that concedes the morality of Marxist socialism, which says that business doesn't have the moral right to be free, that Capitalism is immoral.

Concede this premise long enough, and Liberal corruption will collapse into Marxist socialism, which nobody really wants, other than a fringe group of far-Left radicals who are too naïve and foolish to realize that Marxist socialism was just supposed to be a phantom carrot and stick to funnel Capitalist money into Liberal distribution for the benefit of rich Liberals.

I repeat: Nobody wants Marxist socialism, because then Max EE is not achieved, the money output declines, for example, from a $20 trillion economy to a $2 trillion economy, and then the nice standard of living for the middle class goes away, and there isn't even any money to give as charity to the poor because all the money goes up in smoke, and everyone is sad, angry and miserable. Like the poor nations behind the Iron Curtain in the Communist Russian USSR, which history shows was a horror story of poverty and corruption, with all political dissidents jailed or shot and killed.

Living on a communal farm and growing your own food and knitting your own clothes and smoking cannabis all day and never using money or trade (and never bathing or showering, and never having to take a bath or shower), is a nice way for a bunch of college kids to spend a summer, but it is no way to run a major economy with hundreds of millions of people. It won't pay for the elderly to retire, it won't pay for the young to be educated, and it won't pay for food on the table. Capitalism makes stuff, and gives people jobs, and enables people to buy stuff, and creates opportunity (by making the money that pays for new opportunity), and, yes, we humans are physical, material beings, and having stuff, owning things, making money, having money, spending money, makes us happy, so Capitalism is ethical, Capitalism is good. Because life is good. Being alive is good. So we must set Capitalism free.

And to those Marxist socialists who say that Capitalism leaves us feeling empty, that we are alienated from our own souls, that money can't buy happiness: no, money does not directly buy happiness, it's not like there's a happiness store where you pay $100 and are given the meaning of life in return, but it buys you the time and the means to live your life, thereby giving you the opportunity to find something that means something to you and which can make you happy. Like money paying for a nice wedding dress: the wedding is what matters, not the dress, but the dress is a nice picture frame for the picture of the wedding, metaphorally speaking. The Grinch can't steal Christmas, but you should still use giving Christmas presents in order to show your Christmas love and affection, because opening the presents gives joy to people. Money is a means, not an end, but, absent having means, having power, people would be helpless and powerless, and have nothing.

Voters like integrity, and activists like ideals and honor. Corruption attracts Reformers, and Crusades for Reform are inevitable. The corruption of Liberalism will collapse under the weight of its own contradictions. And, if Marxist socialism is the only option, it would be that which would win. So Ayn Rand (and Murray Rothbard) created the Liberty Movement, where we have ideals and ethics and heroes to believe in, for Capitalism, and for free market economics. Not as a necessary evil, but as a noble ideal.

The historical inevitability of Liberty can be proven in this way: Liberty will have a higher PAMM than Marxist socialism, and so a Libertarian future will pay for itself to come into being over and against a Marxist socialist alternative. However, while a Liberal economy might have the same PAMM as Liberty, it achieves this only by paying bribes and political corruption as the cost of letting free market capitalism have a sphere of freedom within which business can operate.

Corruption is anathema to the human soul, and the hearts and minds of human voters will not tolerate a permanently corrupt political solution, so that, because Liberty is consistent and has integrity in its freedom-based laws, while Liberalism suffers a contradiction between the economic need for freedom and its commitment to controlling and manipulative and freedom-restricting laws and regulations, the ethics and honor of the voters and political activists will prefer Liberty to Liberalism, and so Liberty would win long-term against both Marxist socialism and Liberalism, as a matter of historical necessity.

The Coase Theorem scenarios can be explained by L&E1. For example P internalizes R's positive and negative externalities. P is forced to pay R so that P will suffer the negative externalities of his pollution or of taking his radio broadcast license. P did something bad to a third party, which is the quintessential negative externality, so P must be punished by bearing R's cost.

It is also possible to explain all scenarios entirely by reference to L&E2 alone, to achieve the Max EE outcome, without any reference in the explanation to internalizing negative or positive externalities or transaction costs. Of course the Max EE is not achieved unless the two sides can trade and buy and sell benefits and costs. The transaction costs must be zero for this condition to be met. But L&E1 is often intended merely to let regulators impose the result they subjectively believe would have happened if there had been zero transaction costs and all externalities were internalized.

The key insight from L&E2 is that whether P should be blocked or allowed to proceed depends upon which option produces Max EE, and that Max

EE is achieved if in the first instance the license is given to the radio station with the highest PAMM or if P is allowed to pollute even without cost redistribution to R. By a similar extension of analysis, a voter should, and eventually all voters will, choose Liberty over Liberalism. Because it is Max EE. Liberty will never make less money or be less Capitalistic than Liberalism, but it has more ethics and honor and integrity, which is worth at least \$1 more, so Liberty is always superior to Liberalism.

We conclude this section with nice examples that contrast L&E1 with L&E2, with our first example using cigarettes. L&E1 might tell regulators to tax cigarettes to pay for smoker healthcare costs to internalize the negative externalities of smoking, where the negative externality is that society pays for the healthcare system that treats the health consequences of the smoker's self-destructive behavior, because hospitals will not turn smokers away for inability to pay (given the unrealistic assumption that government will give smokers' tax dollars to hospitals in ratio to healthcare services rendered).

L&E2 might say Max EE is achieved if we either let each smoker pay for his own individual healthcare costs or else let him die and spend no marginal additional cost of healthcare. Taxing cigarettes raises prices, which runs contrary to economic efficiency, whereas the L&E2 solution caps cost as equal to the PAMM lost from each smoker's death.

Another example, which is not so nice, is public education. Suppose that a politician is thinking about things, and she thinks, when a child is educated that benefits society, therefore education has positive externalities, so she thinks in her subjective opinion that if zero transaction costs existed then everyone would willingly pay for every child's tuition, and she uses that unproven subjective feeling as her basis to raise taxes and make every college and university tuition-free. That is an example of how L&E1 works, in practice.

L&E2 might say, completely deregulate and privatize all education, and then whatever is the order that emerges naturally from the chaos will be the maximum economically efficient outcome, because that is how economics works.

L&E1 says that zero transaction costs are impossible, but the economy should have what would happen if they existed, so government must guess what that outcome would be and impose it onto everyone by force.

L&E2 says no, that is a misinterpretation of C/C. Let people be as free as possible, and the Max EE outcome will arise naturally. It will arise precisely because it has more PAMM to spend to bring itself into being than any alternative scenario. We might not have perfect zero transaction costs, but no reason exists why P cannot pay R, no legal or practical barrier constrains P, in a multitude of situations, so the theory of L&E2 can and will work.

One can do some interesting things with L&E2, such as, for example, solving the Israel-Palestine problem. If the value of the Palestinian land is more valuable to Israel then to Palestine, then the Jews would pay the Palestinians the cost of having that land, namely, by paying the cost for the Palestinians to pack up and move and buy some nice land somewhere else and go somewhere else, and then the Jews could claim all that land for Israel, and the Palestinians would (be paid to) fully consent and agree, and the Jews could spend an amount of money equal to the difference between the benefit of that land to the Jews, compared to the benefit of that land to the Palestinians, in order to do so. But, if the cost exceeded the benefit, and the Jews could not do so, then the Max EE Result would be to get the Israelis out of the Palestinian-held lands, and let the Palestinians form their own state. Economics, and relative costs and benefits, would dictate the proper solution.

Similar thinking can be applied across a broad range of problems, for example, let the Pro-Lifers pay pregnant women to bear their babies, and, if they don't choose to pay the cost of the pregnancy that they demand to let happen, by paying the costs of having the baby and raising the child, plus a bonus bounty to pay the woman in order to compensate her for choosing childbirth. Then also give the woman the freedom to have an abortion, if the Pro-Lifers won't pay the Cost of pregnancy, because the Pro-Choice result is what would happen absent the Pro-Life objection. And so on.

In this way, Coase Theorem can solve many thorny policy debates using a precisely logical, mathematical, economic approach, which is purely objective and deductive, and not subjective or emotional. It is textbook Libertarian economics that TANSTAAFL, "there ain't no such thing as a free lunch," so, if you want a benefit for yourself from something that you will force onto someone else, you should pay for it, to internalize the negative externality.

The Liberal Conservative status quo has naturally arisen from the class warfare between capitalism and Marxist socialism according to the economic principles outlined above. Emerging fro the Industrial Revolution, it maximized profit and PAMM and AMM for capitalism to exist, but the corrupt states and nations and governments, which had evolved from the kingdoms and feudal estates of the past, demanded payment as a cost of allowing freedom to exist.

This naturally evolved into the Liberal government corruption we see today, where the rich get freedom in return for paying million dollar fines to regulators for breaking the law and bribing politicians through lobbying and corruption and the rich then do whatever they want while the middle class gets screwed over and the middle class is at the same time then confined by the laws and regulations which no longer apply to the rich.

The rich and the politicians become the ruling

class, while the middle class and the poor are second-class citizens, and the more this Liberal system works, the more corrupt it becomes. But it is institutionalized corruption, and so cannot survive, because it will kindle in the hearts of humans a fervent desire to abolish it, because humans are good and ethical naturally, and good will always triumph over evil in the end. So the corrupt Liberal state is doomed.

But Marxist socialism does not maximize PAMM and so it too will never survive. The survival of the human species still depends on making as much money as possible, so humans will never choose socialism, and, even if they did, it would go bankrupt and collapse, much as the USSR did against the Capitalism of Reagan and Thatcher.

The only system which maximizes PAMM and AMM, thereby paying for itself to come into existence by affording to pay the cost to defeat any lesser-PAMM system and still take a profit on its existence for society, while at the same time having moral integrity and ethics and honor and internal consistency and coherence, by being capable of honest law-abiding behavior by all system participants, is Libertarianism and Anarcho-Capitalism.

For example:

Capitalism: $20 trillion.

Marxist socialism: $2 trillion.

The Liberty movement, taking a loan today from future generations, could afford to spend up to almost $18 trillion in order to win, while the Marxist socialists could only spend up to $2 trillion. So Liberty must win.

Against Liberalism, even assuming a net $20 trillion AMM compared to Liberty either way, Liberty has one benefit, ethics and honor and integrity, because people need to be free and it lets people be free, as compared to the corruption of Liberalism, where people need to be free but it says people should be taxed and regulated so people use corruption to steal the freedom that they require in order to survive and so, PAMM being even, other than the people who benefit from the way Liberals distribute wealth, namely, the very corrupt politicians and the very poor incompetents who rely on the welfare state for their survival, no one likes Liberalism, and nobody wants Liberal corruption.

The great innovation of the Liberty movement, which did not exist before today, is that it achieves Max EE plus moral integrity. This is a combination that voters will tend to choose, in comparison to political corruption, over a long enough time line, because ethics is inherently more desirable than corruption, for human beings. So Liberty will win.

In Liberty, everyone is free to achieve Max EE, so there is no need for corruption as a cost of Max EE, and everyone is free to pursue their natural economic self-interest. At the same time, if rights are assigned in the first instance to the individual, not to society, then the poor and the working class does not get screwed over, as, for example, going back to Coase Theorem, P must pay R the cost to R for P's conduct, such that both P and R are better off, because the Liberty legal system begins with the assumption that R owns R's body and R's health, and therefore P would lack the right to violate R's property absent paying R for R's consent to do so.

Because both P and R are better off for having made the deal, we assume that P and R will freely choose the deal because they are motivated to maximize profit by their economic self-interest, and so freedom in Liberty becomes a perfect system that everyone can abide by and which everyone becomes the better off for. Ultimately, Libertarian deregulation and economic freedom is the practical application of the condition of zero transaction costs, because everyone is free to shift money to pay for costs of benefits.

As such, the Liberty Movement's historical rise and eventual triumph is inevitable. You, the Liberals and Conservatives and Marxist socialists, give up. Resistance is futile. You will be assimilated. Liberty will win. We will win.

WHAT IS THE LIBERTARIAN AXIOM?

Most libertarians would point to the principle that one should never initiate violence, and use force only for self defense, as the core axiom for liberty—the axiom that I call NVP, the Non-Violence Principle. Here I write to propose a second axiom, based on some recent conversation with my fellow Libertarian Party members.

I know one LP member who opposes big government except for public education to give poor kids a leg up. I know another who opposes big government except for Social Security for retirees, on the belief it isn't fair to deny someone benefits they paid into for decades. I know a third who opposes big government except for welfare and food stamps for the very poor. This person is convinced that a Marxist revolution will happen if all welfare is cut. I have also heard a Libertarian talk about the "real" pain and suffering of the poor that is alleviated by welfare, as if the pain caused by big government is not equally real.

These people, and I now suspect most Americans, understand libertarian economics, but they think that theft (in the form of taxation) is justified if it is for a good, worthy cause. Each person has his own pet cause that he wants government to fund, even while wanting taxes cut to pay for anything else. There are Social Conservatives who crusade for freedom and want freedom for everyone, except for the freedom for pregnant mothers to abort or for LGBTs to exist, because they think gay sex and abortion are sins, and the ends justify a limitation or compromise of (other people's) freedom. Everyone wants freedom, they just don't want absolute freedom.

But we Libertarians really do want absolute freedom.

I propose a new axiom: that the ends never justify the means. Good ends do not justify evil means. I term this the Anti-Marxist Axiom.

If you believe this, then theft (taxation) is never justified, even for the noblest purpose, and even if the rich have more money than they need. My justification for this axiom is moral, not pragmatic, and, in a weird way, Kantian. Kant's signature contribution to ethics is the theory of the Categorical Imperative, which I interpret to mean that, for something to be good, it must be right at all times and places universally. If there is an exception to an ethical (or political) principle then it was not rational or true, it was merely an expediency of the moment.

To be a coherent theory, libertarianism needs the Anti-Marxist Axiom, otherwise it is just a rule of thumb to be compromised or abandoned when someone feels justified in doing so. If you use evil means to achieve good ends, logically the result will not be ethical, because you conceded to evil in order to achieve your goal.

If you want to fund a good cause with taxes then you conceded the validity of statism. If you accept that people make and earn money, and thereby morally deserve to own wealth, and then say that you can take someone's money away from them to spend as you see fit, even for a good cause, you have conceded and condoned widespread systemic theft. It should not then surprise you that a bunch of crooks, literally thieves, actual criminals, will run for office to acquire this opportunity and then will raise taxes on you to pay for evil things while spouting all sorts of virtuous good causes to justify it.

There is a saying "power corrupts, and power attracts the corruptible." (Attributed to Frank Herbert.) I can say something similar: theft attracts criminals. This is a necessary and sufficient explanation for why big government is evil and will always become evil even if it begins as good.

Absent this axiom, you will find good cause after good cause, requiring tax raise after tax raise, and more and more theft to pay for your virtuous plans, until, from a libertarian starting point, you inevitably collapse into socialism. Either you have a universal, absolute axiom, or you face a very realistic slippery slope—even if sliding down it takes a nation 200 years.

Libertarians should consider abandoning their pet causes and commit to the Anti-Marx Axiom, to protect the purity of our principles. Libertarianism as a political theory needs an axiom, a self-evident principle to justify itself. If it does not have a principle then it is not a theory, it would be a mere pragmatic movement, or merely a feeling that government is bad. NVP is a good axiom, but many libertarians feel justified in making exceptions. The axiom that the ends never justify the means says there are no exceptions. If people want compromise, let them vote for the establishment. If they want principled politics, then they should vote for us. But how can we be a party of principles if we don't know what our core principle is?

THE MATHEMATICAL ARGUMENT FOR WHY LIBERTARIANISM WILL END POVERTY

Being a big fan of Friedrich Nietzsche, I have a fondness for clever, memorable aphorisms, on the model of his "All that which does not kill me makes me stronger," which is one of my personal mottos. One such aphorism is: "Socialists believe that no one should own anything. Libertarians believe that everyone should own something." What this aphorism gets at, among other things, is that both socialists and libertarians have an answer to the problem of poverty, but our answer differs sharply from theirs. In terms of the political appeal of libertarianism, this is an important point to hammer home to voters.

The leftists and socialists say that they want to help the poor and that the libertarians and conservatives are the enemies of the working class and we don't care about the poor. This naturally drives working class voters to vote Democrat when they should be voting Libertarian. I can't speak for conservatives, and I can't speak for other libertarians either. But, speaking for myself, I can say that I do care about the poor, and my brand of libertarianism, which comes from a liberal-tarian or neo-liberal strain, is very intently focused upon ending poverty. Poverty eradication is one of my goals. It is not the only goal. But it is a valid goal, and it is an achievable goal.

I would tell voters that libertarianism will end world poverty. That is a bold claim, and I expect most voters would reply: "Why? And how?" One answer can be found in my unique reinterpretation and application of the business management philosophy called Six Sigma.

Six Sigma is a technique developed in the manufacturing industry, and it is widely credited with the high quality of electronics devices that are manufactured today. Six Sigma is a mathematical approach to business management and products manufacturing, which states that hard math and statistics should be used to manage a business and to control the work product of a factory. The key mathematical equation used by Six Sigma practitioners, which I would like you to understand, is: $Y = f(X) + e$, where X represents input, $f(X)$ represents the process that is applied to the input, Y represents the output, and e represents the errors and imperfections inherent in human existence.

The core teaching of Six Sigma is that most business processes are inefficient and generate waste, and vast amounts of money can be saved by redesigning the process to eliminate waste. The Six Sigma process analyzes the X and the $f(X)$ in order to find the most efficient method of achieving the desired Y. The Six Sigma process uses math and science to find the best process to achieve efficiency, quality and success. Six Sigma believes that with the exact same input X, e.g. with the same amount of work, labor, effort, and raw materials, the output Y can be very different if the process, the $f(X)$, is different. What matters is the $f(X)$, not the X, because you need a good process to get the most output out of your input.

Six Sigma is not mere abstract theory. It has been used in practical reality, for example by Motorola, Bank of America, and major car manufacturers in Detroit. The data suggests that when a Fortune 500 company implements Six Sigma, and when they do it correctly, and especially when they use it on their manufacturing processes and factories, on average their net profits increase by as much as one billion dollars per year.

Now, let me get to the main argument in this essay. We can consider a national economy to be akin to a business or a factory. The work that people do, and the natural resources and raw materials that go into their work, are the input. The money that is made and the consumable goods and services that they produce are the output. And the political system, be it libertarian capitalism or socialist left-liberalism, is the process which takes inputs and creates outputs. My argument is that the process of heavy government intervention in the economy, pioneered by the New Deal and implemented by Obama and the Democrats today, is very wasteful. If Motorola could save a billion dollars by more efficient processes, then the United States of America could probably save trillions of dollars by a more efficient politico-economic process.

And the trillions of dollars of added wealth would end up in the hands of the people, of the working class. I fully believe that if all the economic waste was eliminated, in the USA and also if the rest of the world implemented free market economics, then the added wealth would be enough to end poverty, so that the vast majority of humans would achieve a middle class or upper class standard of living.

Why would capitalism be a more efficient economic system than Democratic left-liberalism? The answer to that question is so big that it is beyond the scope of this article. In my nonfiction book "Golden Rule Libertarianism," I take 100 pages to explain why a system of money and prices and free choices among competing businesses is the best way to coordinate the diverse economic activity of billions of different producers and consumers in a division of labor economy. The arguments in my book can be called the Hasanian answer. There is also the Randian answer, the Rothbardian answer, the Milton Friedman answer, etc. Between you and I, let's both of us take it for granted, for the sake of my argument, and leave the details for a different discussion.

Why would libertarianism put money in the hands of the poor and middle class, as opposed to the rich? As a factual matter, the government spends trillions of dollars taken from the taxpayers, so if you end the tax and spend leftist policies, then that money remains in the taxpayers' hands, to be spent by the people. Of course, leftists claim that the rich are the ones who pay taxes, and that tax and spend helps the poor.

However, in fact, the lower class and middle class bear a tax burden that is far worse than the taxes actually paid by the rich. This is because of the low tax rates for long-term capital gains and dividends, where the rich get their money, and the ability of the rich to hold their money in offshore tax shelters, which enable the rich to avoid paying taxes, as well as the tax burdens that target the poor, such as the property tax and the sales tax, social security withholding as a tax, and also the high tax brackets for middle class salaries. $1000 is a ton of money for a working class person or a middle class person, whereas one million dollars is meaningless to a billionaire, so taxes hit the lower class with a proportionate impact far higher than they hit the upper class. The working class and middle class actually are the ones hit hardest by taxation, while the rich find ways to avoid paying taxes, or can afford to pay the taxes they pay. Given that this is true, tax cuts actually help the working class and middle class and have minimal direct benefits for the rich.

A libertarian Six Sigma approach would eliminate the waste in government spending, creating huge savings for the American people. In terms of hard data, the United States government, including the combined federal, state, and local governments, are the biggest spenders of the taxpayers' money, and the examples of bureaucratic failure, waste, and incompetence in government spending are too many to list. There are bridges to nowhere, statues built for no reason, railroad lines constructed that nobody wants to use, all costing the taxpayers billion upon billion.

The government is necessarily inefficient, because the government does not need to compete against someone else to satisfy people, and people are forced to accept what the government does, so competition does not exist to hold bureaucrats accountable and force them to do what the people want. Simply be eliminating all government waste, at both the federal, state, and local levels, we could probably save four trillion dollars of Americans' hard-earned money. Then, if you let people be free to be productive, and you unlock the money-making potential of every worker, especially the highly intelligent and creative people, and if you give people broad freedom to trade with other people without regulatory controls, I believe that another $4 trillion would be added to GDP. $4 trillion plus $4 trillion is $8 trillion.

The US GDP is roughly $20 trillion in circa 2020 (Source: Google and Wikipedia), and it is plausible to think that if we replace a bad, flawed $f(X)$ with a good, efficient, waste-free $f(X)$ then Y could vastly increase, which is in line with what Six Sigma improvements have achieved for businesses that replace bad processes with good processes. So Liberty pays for itself. In terms of Six Sigma using math and science to discover the correct process for a business, which is a core tenet of Six Sigma, I think that the work done by Milton Friedman, who completed an exhaustive, thorough scientific research using hard data and statistical math to show that capitalist-leaning economies generate more wealth than socialist-leaning economies, is true to the Six Sigma approach of statistical analysis. So my application of Six Sigma would take it as a given, proven by the libertarian economists, that the libertarian process is the right one to use to redesign the economy.

Let us consider the number I mentioned: eight trillion dollars recovered due to libertarian policies. America has about 300 million citizens. Let's assume that the poorest 90 percent comprise 270 million people. If we eliminated economic waste and save or create eight trillion dollars, and divide that amongst 270 million people, and just give them the money as a "negative income tax," to use a phrase from Libertarian economist Milton Friedman, then each poor and middle class person would get an additional $29,600 a year. That would give a reasonable amount of money, enough to live a decent, happy life, to each and every working class person in the USA.

Note that, if we eliminate most regulations on the economy, then, because regulations focused on safety tend to make things more expensive, deregulation will make everything cheaper to buy, so when I assert $29,600 more for each poor person I think that when adjusted for real purchasing power every poor person will achieve middle class buying power.

We would lift the poor out of poverty, using a mathematical Six Sigma methodology focused on redesigning the process to eliminate waste and improve efficiency, which experience has already proven to be highly effective in the business world. We could end poverty by using reason and logic, instead of the mushy illogical stupidity of the Left. I conclude by repeating the same point I opened with: Libertarians are not the enemies of the poor and the working class, we are their best friends with their best interests at heart. The leftist Democrat poor don't understand this, but we would be well advised to teach this to the working class voters. Remember the aphorism: Socialists believe that no one should own anything. Libertarians believe that everyone should own something. And our policies will create the new wealth for the poor to claim as their own private property.

TO WORLD PEACE: THE PRINCIPLE OF ETHNIC SOVEREIGNTY

(Author's note: This was written in 2015, so some of the references are dated, but the principles are still relevant and remain the same, and will still apply 10,000 years from today!)

What do the recent Black people vs. white police race riots in St. Louis, the recent Israeli vs. Palestinian conflict, and the Russian annexation of East Ukraine, and the US military operations against ISIS in Iraq and Syria, all have in common? My answer is that these crises were all caused by the same problem, and they could all be solved by one solution. This solution, which I call the principle of ethnic sovereignty, is something that I propose as a giant step in the direction of achieving world peace, and an end to all wars. Libertarians are generally antiwar pacifists, and my theory will be of particular interest to libertarian doves.

What is the principle of ethnic sovereignty? To explain it, I must begin with a personal anecdote. I was born and raised in New York, but my father is an immigrant from Bangladesh, which is a small, poor nation in southeast Asia, and I have been taught Bangladeshi ethnic identity my entire life. Bangladesh was a part of the British colony of India. When the Indian resistance movement, led by Gandhi, was finally able to drive the British Empire out, the lands of the colony of India were divided up into new nations. The modern country of India was created, and all Hindu people were forced to move to India. In the west, Pakistan was created, and in the east, East Pakistan was created, to be governed by West Pakistan. The Muslims were forced to move to West Pakistan or East Pakistan. The political leaders who partitioned India and Pakistan believed that if the people of a nation shared one religion then they would get along and be unified. India would be Hindu, and Pakistan would by Islamic.

But in the case of Pakistan and East Pakistan, this religious unity failed to come true. The people in West Pakistan spoke the language of Urdu, and were ethnic Pakistanis. The people in East Pakistan spoke a different language, called Bangla, and we were ethnic Bangladeshis. Bangladesh has a strong cultural identity, dating back to a rich tradition of literature and music, and the Pakistani culture was completely different from the Bangladeshi ethnic culture.

The Pakistanis grew angry at Bangladeshi culture, which was different from the Pakistani culture embraced by Pakistan's leaders, and the Pakistan government used aggressive force to suppress Bangla culture and to seek to impose Pakistani culture onto the ethnic Bangladeshis in East Pakistan. We, of course, did not like this, and the cultural animosity evolved into a political movement aimed at liberating East Pakistan from Pakistani control. East Pakistan called itself Bangladesh, and Bangladesh eventually began a War of Independence against Pakistan. Many Bangladeshis, including members of my family, died in the conflict. In the end, with help from allies in India and the West, Bangladesh won the War of Independence, and was set free as its own country. In the 1960's, The Beatles played a concert to raise money to support the Bangladeshi War of Independence, so even The Beatles cared.

What lessons can we learn from the story of Bangladesh and Pakistan? I draw a broad conclusion, which is that when an ethnic group occupies a geographic region, those people are going to want to be free, and to rule themselves in democratic self-government, and if you let people from a different ethnic group, in a different region, rule over a people from afar, then you are asking for war. It is natural and inevitable for an ethnic group to fight for freedom if they are being rule by a different ethnic group.

Generally, if every ethnic group on planet Earth was given sovereign rule over the territory that it occupies, if all national borders were redrawn so that each ethnic group had self-government, then I believe that we would be one giant step closer to world peace. In terms of right and wrong, I think that each people has the right to be governed by themselves, because when you let a different group govern them, this is tantamount to tyranny and oppression, whereas self-government is a vital component of freedom, as America's founding fathers knew when they rebelled against the British Empire.

How would the principle of ethnic sovereignty solve the world crises I listed above? The application of the solution to the problems, listed in order, is: the police who impose order are a part of the government that governs an area. If the ethnic group in a community is African American, then they should have African American police to govern them, to give them political sovereignty. The data shows that the St. Louis suburb where the race riots are happening is 85% African American yet almost the entire police force is white (and the local politicians are all white too).

White racist conservatives may say that the Equal Protection Clause forbids letting police recruiters in black areas favor blacks, and that race blindness is the proper solution to the problem. I reject this argument, despite the fact that I like race blindness as an antidote to racism, because the actual text of the Constitution says only that everyone should have equal protection under the laws, so that if whites are protected by white policemen, the equal protection of the law for blacks would actually be for blacks to be protected by Black policemen. Draw police recruits and political appointees from the community that they will be protecting or serving, and you end a lot of the impetus for race riots and civil rights struggles.

Note that I am not advocating redrawing the city and state lines within the USA for each ethnic group to rule its own areas, but that, within the context of the unity in the United States, our goal should be for each area within the US be under the control of its own people, be they blacks, Hispanic immigrants, Irish Catholics, etc.

In the East Ukraine crisis, instead of making Ukraine into an issue in the conflict between the USA and Russia, simply let each region be governed by its own people. This would let the ethnic Russians in East Ukraine join Russia if they wish. But, by the same principle, you then draw a line around the non-Russian Ukrainians in Ukraine, and you use the NATO military to prevent Russia from conquering non-Russian ethnic territory. Under the principle of ethnic sovereignty, the borders of nations drawn on a map are not a game for the rulers of the world to play, using people and soldiers as pawns in a global game of chess. Instead, the lines of the maps become an exercise in designing freedom for each group of people on the planet.

Regarding ISIS, it is widely understood that ISIS rose to power by appealing to the Sunni Muslims in Iraq and Syria, who were oppressed by the Shiite Muslims in Syria and ignored by the Shiite Muslim government in Iraq. The United States, like the world rulers dating back to the British Empire, consider the lines of national borders to be inviolate, even if two rival ethnic groups are trapped within the same national boundaries. I say, redraw the lines, and break Iraq into a Shiite South, a Sunni North, and a Kurdish Northeast. But, in each region, create strong ties of trade with the USA, and seek to give the new nations a government modeled on the freedom and individual rights of American-style government.

And, in Syria, recognize the Syrian rebels as a government, and let the Sunni Muslims govern the Sunni Muslims, while opposing the Shiite dictatorship of Assad. It is too late to do this in time to stop ISIS, but, if the United States does the right thing and leads a military operation to defeat ISIS, then this redrawing of the lines on the map for freedom and democracy is necessary to stabilize the Iraqi region. (Note that it is perfectly appropriate for the USA to use military force to defeat ISIS, because ISIS has made it clear that they intend a terrorist attack against us, so this is the legitimate use of force for national self-defense.)

I conclude with the most politically sensitive issue, Israel and Palestine. On my mother's side of the family I am ethnically Jewish, and I believe that the state of Israel has every right to exist. If you look back 5000 years earlier in human history, Israel belonged to the Jews, it was taken from us by force over and over again, by the Egyptians, the Babylonians, the Romans, and the Medieval forces which controlled it during the Middle Ages. Despite this, however, the Palestinians are a different ethnic group, and they occupy a distinct geographical scope, in the West Bank and the Gaza Strip.

The state of Israel has no right to prevent the Palestinians from forming their own Palestinian state, nor does the state of Israel have the right to regulate or control the Palestinians within their own borders, nor to blockade the Palestinian border, and it is none of Israel's business whom the Palestinians choose to act as the government of Palestine. Israel may defend itself from Palestine if Palestinian terrorists attack, but this right begins and ends at the border between Israel and Palestine. So long as the Israelis behave as though they own Palestine and have the right to control it, so long as the Israelis refuse to recognize the state of Palestine, and while Israel denies to the Palestinian people the right of ethnic sovereignty, the Palestinians will know that they are being treated like slaves or dogs by the Israelis. In this condition, the Palestinians will rebel, and fight for freedom, as is their right.

Instead of one state, if we had two states, an Israel that minds its own business, and a free Palestine, then the Israel-Palestine conflict can, and will, be extinguished, because nobody will have any motive to fight any longer, and everyone will get what they want. The right-wing bigots of the Israeli Right will say that this would constitute the Jews surrendering to the Palestinian terrorists. The terrorists have sinned, I will concede that. But two wrongs don't make a right, and an ethnic group of people still deserves its freedom even if some of them fight for freedom using evil methods. Also note that, while all the Palestinian land could rightfully be claimed as part of Israel, I think the generous and charitable move by Israel would be to gift that small slice of land to Palestine, and not begrudge it or seek to retake it. The Torah states "Love thy neighbor as thyself," and the Palestinians are, quite literally, Israel's neighbors.

During the 1800s and early 1900s, the European colonial powers, including Britain, France, and Belgium, especially in dealing with their colonies in Africa and the Middle East, developed an explicit policy of sowing strife and discord by taking different ethnic groups that disliked each other and trapping them within one nation within the borders they drew on the map. This is why, in Africa, many nations contain warring African tribes, and why in the Middle East countries there are opposing Sunni and Shiite sects of Muslims who hate each other within one nation. The colonial powers knew that the ethnic groups would fight each other, seeking their freedom, which would weaken them and make them easier to rule by the Western empires.

Indeed, I would define the idea that one ethnic group should rule another ethnic group as a fundamentally colonial idea, which should have been discredited by now in our post-colonial age of democracy. I can say, as a Bangladeshi, that each ethnic group which lives in a geographic region will naturally chafe at foreign control, and will seek the freedom of democratic self-government. It is natural for freedom fighters to fight, and to die, and to kill, for their ideal of freedom. We must abandon the colonial attitude that the national boundaries of borders drawn on the maps are sacrosanct. Instead, let's redraw the lines on the map so that each ethnic group owns its own nation. Give the peoples of the world their freedom, and you pave the path to world peace. And what ideal to fight for is there that is any better than world peace?

So I would define the principle of ethnic sovereignty as the statement that each geographical ethnic group dominant in one region should have the right to political autonomy and democratic self-government. But what, then, if an ethnic group becomes a tyranny or dictatorship, and seeks to repress the rights of the individual or of ethnic minorities or racial minorities in that area? Then the oppressed person should simply get up and leave, and move to somewhere else, where they can be free and live life as they want. The Pilgrims and Puritans leaving England for religious freedom in Colonial America is a good example.

This is why the principle of ethnic sovereignty

only works if paired with a principle of free, open, and unrestrained immigration borders. Let any individual leave or enter any nation freely, and have a cheap and fast path to citizenship.

No quotas, no visas, no ten-year wait. Just come, apply, pass an two-hour-long multiple choice exam to prove you understand the English language and know how the American political system works, swear to uphold the US Constitution, and become a US citizen. Or move to any other country you want, until you find one you like, where you can be free.

The Conservative will scream in reply: Then they'll all come to America! I say: Let them come. They do no harm to me, nor to you, so we have no right to keep them out.

The Conservative counter: but immigrants from poor countries, who are uneducated and unskilled, drain the United States welfare system, raising taxes on the middle class. I say: Then end the welfare system. That is the only correct solution. Closed borders and choking immigration is not the correct solution. Either let them in and end the welfare state, or let them in and eat the higher taxes. But don't keep them out. Otherwise they are trapped in the foreign dictatorship, which is an insult to freedom and liberty everywhere, including here, and an insult to the dignity of all human beings, including you.

For ethnic sovereignty to work, the ethnic majority must not have the ability to trample and violate the rights of individuals in that society. For which the individual must be able to leave at will, and cross borders, for which there must be open borders. Freedom demands ethnic sovereignty, and the open immigration rights to protect the rights of individuals within that ethnic sovereign nation.

MAKING IT WORK: LIBERTARIAN SOLUTIONS IN HEALTHCARE AND PRIVATIZATION

Libertarian policy proposals are often ridiculed for being too impractical and naively idealistic. This article will put forward practical solutions for implementing libertarian policies in ways that can, and will, work in the real world. Privatization and healthcare, two areas in which libertarian policy is hotly contested, are the focus.

I'll start with a summary of two objections to freedom and follow with a solution for overcoming that objection. I will then add details.

First Objection: Infrastructure—such as roads

and train lines—and utilities cannot be privatized because they are natural monopolies: two operators cannot compete along the same line at the same time.

First Solution: If the right to operate the space, be it the road, or train line, or power line, were auctioned off for very short periods, such as 6 to twelve months, at open competitive bidding, it stands to reason that the efficient privatization company would make enough money to place the highest bid at the next round, and would have operated in the best way possible to maximize profits and consumers (if consumers cared to listen to reason). In other words, private operators would compete along the vector of time, not space, with the most efficient one winning the highest profit and likely making the highest bid for the next slot of time.

Second Objection: Under the current system, that evolved under capitalism, health insurers pay for the healthcare of the people who pay healthcare premiums, the premiums bearing no direct relation to the healthcare actually received. The health insurer is the "payer," who pays the doctor, while the person receiving healthcare is the "patient," and there is no direct relationship between payer and patient at the point of sale. The system would have to work this way, because the whole idea of insurance is that you pay for the risk that you may one day need insurance, not for the actual healthcare you receive thereafter. This system causes a disconnect between the healthcare buyers and the healthcare sellers, enabling the sellers to jack up their prices.

The patient is like someone walking into a candy store with the ability to charge anything he wants to someone else's credit card (the payer), and never see the person who owns the credit card. We would expect the candy store to charge exorbitant prices, and the purchaser to get fat on candy, and then sweep the prices under the rug and expect the person who pays for the credit card to clean up the mess and find a way to pay for the candy somehow.

This is a broken system, and the socialists say the solution is "single payer," which would mean that the government would make healthcare public and have socialized medicine, and healthcare will be "free," which really means that the taxpayer, not the patient, will pay for healthcare, and the disconnect between payer and patient will be complete. Only big government and a bunch of crusty, arrogant, elitist bureaucrats have the power to step in and force prices down to affordable levels by setting or capping prices by laws and regulations, because the greedy private health insurers want higher prices to make more money.

Second Solution: To the extent that health insurance as such poses a structural tendency to sever payment from delivery of service, the problem can be solved not by leaning toward big government but by moving toward greater freedom in free market competition. Require doctors to publish schedules of what services they offer and at what costs, as would be reasonable in any capitalist system in which sellers must be honest about what they are selling. Then drastically deregulate health insurers so that any entrepreneur can start a health insurance company and compete in any state, across state lines. In this ideal world, health insurers would compete in a marketplace—not a fake Obamacare Exchange but a real capitalist free market.

What will naturally evolve from this is a situation in which, to pass along as much cost saving to customers as possible, in order to get as much business as possible, some health insurers will develop a system for the insureds to pre-pay for the price services they want, from specific doctors at specific prices. Then, if they get sick and need those services, they will get what they shopped for and paid for. The actual payment mechanism would still be the insurer pooling all payments and then paying after the fact for the people who got sick, but price competition would force doctors to lower their prices to competitive levels to get buyers, and this same pricing pressure would force health insurers to pass along the best deal to the buyer. Premiums would be applied after the fact, pro rata, to the healthcare that people chose to buy before the fact. A buyer will compare prices and choose a seller, and buyers and sellers will naturally converge at the equilibrium price point between supply and demand--which as (smart, sane, rational, libertarian) economists know, is the right antidote for monopolistic price gouging.

Details:

Examples of so-called natural monopolies include transit routes, bandwidth, electric utilities and power lines, cable service, garbage collection, and air space for planes or drones.

"Natural monopoly" public infrastructure can be privatized. And they should be privatized. Most people are aware that public monopolies are often mismanaged by operators who have no accountability to the public.

But it is assumed that there can be no competing alternatives, since the land or space simply isn't there. So let there be a monopoly, but have the government regulate it so it will be forced it to sell at price points below the monopoly price. What this natural monopoly thought process ignores is that there are many ways for companies to compete, if you think outside the box.

Competition in running natural monopoly infrastructure can take place along the dimension of time, not of space, such that, when the natural monopolies are privatized, what is sold is a lease, essentially, to last six to 12 months, but no longer. The buyer would have every right to do whatever he likes with the land or infrastructure and monetize and run it as he pleases, but only for the term of the lease, at which point the right to buy the next period of time would be up for open bidding and awarded to the highest bidder.

Economic efficiency and capitalist theory

dictate that the company that can make the most money from such an enterprise will tend to be both the highest bidder and the company that can continue to run it the best. If a transit route is run badly, sales will flag, profits will drop, and the opportunity will arise for someone better to place a higher bid in the next round. Thus, even with only one owner, there will be competition in the economic sense.

Additions to the scheme may need to be made, such as requiring a pro rata portion of an operator's profits to be paid back to previous owners who invested in long-term durable equipment or improvements from which the current owner benefits. But such additions are not difficult to design. As a bonus, if any contractor commits massive fraud against the consumer, this will be easy to see, because if a competing operator wins the next lease bid, when he looks at the infrastructure he will see what the previous operator did to it, and consumers will be protected better than we would be under heavy regulator scrutiny.

Today's economy already proves that this will work. There are hundreds of huge corporations that buy some downstream service from only one seller, for the term of a lease; and there is ample price competition, even though only one seller can get the deal to be a supplier at one time. The companies that sell "back end" human resources (HR) services (outsourced services such as paychecks and benefits management) to Fortune 500 corporations are an example: a buyer can sensibly go with only one seller at a time, but there is a ton of competition. Another example: Places exist where various owners own the rights to different heights above the ground of a single plot of land, so that two companies can compete by owning different floors of the same building, competing along the dimension of height, not of length.

The person who made the original objection to privatization will object again, saying that the rich will bid big to get ownership of the monopoly, charge high prices while offering crappy service, and run away after their lease ends--taking profits derived from forcing people to pay a lot for a service with no alternatives. The operators' costs would have been low, since they didn't give a damn about infrastructure investments. But this objection reduces merely to the general argument against free market capitalism. The Marxists and socialists think that rich people get rich by fleecing their victims. If you believe instead, as smart people do, that money is made in a free society by creating high quality at an affordable price where supply meets demand, then the objection collapses. Specifically it is wrong because an operator who does a good job will always make more, net, long term, than a con artist;, hence the good operator will have more money and more motivation to outbid the crooks.

This is not to say that the system can never be abused. No system is perfect. Privatization is certainly not less perfect that a regulated natural monopoly, and it would ultimately be far better. Just ask anyone who rides the subway in New York City: in addition to being a vital means of transportation for millions of New Yorkers, it is also the location that the wonderfully brainless liberal politicians of New York have chosen as the de facto living space for the mentally ill homeless people, just to get them off the streets. The bigger picture is that the economic demand for the subway would justify a rise in fares that is politically unpopular and therefore impossible.

So New York City as subway operator does not, and cannot, spend the money it should to maintain the subway service as it deserves and needs. The New York Times even ran a crusade to get more spending for the subways, noting how horrible they are and how many people use them, which crusade did not succeed, and could not succeed. The free market would do better.

I have suggested six to 12 months as the basic contract period for the operation of natural monopolies; it could be two or three years, but it needs to be short enough to enable consumers to hold bad operators accountable so that better ones can step in. Employees may not want six or 12 month contracts, and somewhat more may need to be paid them on this account. Nevertheless, we need to get away from the labor union mentality, according to which the labor pool only works if employees are chained to their jobs and employers are chained to long-term labor contracts.

The United States is becoming "the gig economy," as they say; led by the Uber and Lyft drivers. A lot of industries are moving toward hiring employees for a temporary, shorter duration and away from hiring them for permanent, full-time jobs. Employees with strong professional skills are so valuable that no one who purchased a short-term lease on a natural monopoly would want to get rid of them.

As far as planning goes, there are examples in today's economy of businesses drawing up plans for long-term operations, because that is how they can best succeed, but if their basic contracts are not renewed, they just tear up the plans. In business you need long-term plans, but you also need to face the risk that these plans may fail dramatically, at any time.

If you don't get investors in your second year of operation, you just eat the third, fourth and fifth years of your business plan, no matter how great those years might have been.

Now to some details about healthcare. Free market economics doesn't work if there is a disconnect between the person who pays the money for a benefit and the person who receives the benefit. The disconnect causes prices and costs to skyrocket, because the buyer cannot force the seller down. Many libertarians already know this: one of our objections to government spending is that the government will overspend because there is a disconnect between the taxpayer and the beneficiary. Healthcare, where the health insurer pays but the patient receives the treatment, and does not directly pay the doctor, and the doctors don't compete for each individual patient on price, is a great example of a buy-sell disconnect.

The problem with health insurance is that, originally, it was in fact insurance that a person bought to mitigate the risk of getting sick, but it has become a behemoth that pays for all medical expenses and then collects exorbitant and arbitrary amounts from the public, with no connection between payments and collections in an individual patient's case. The problem arises because, by the time people become sick, their medical costs are typically too great for them to pay, so they must have already had insurance to get treatment, and the insurance will then end up paying all costs.

To reform healthcare, first, require doctors, as a condition of receiving their license to practice medicine, or merely by means of laws mandating truth in advertising, to create a schedule of fees and prices for each of their services, and publish it, and let individual patients receive that care if they pay that fee from the schedule of rates. Second, break up the regulations of health insurance companies so that anyone can start one and can compete in every state with a minimum of red tape. Third, require that each health insurer publish the actuarial tables that each insurer is using, showing what portion of your payment will pay for what medical treatment in the future from what doctor's schedule of fees.

Fourth, allow the consumer to "buy" his future medical treatment by choosing what portion of his premium he chooses to allocate to the doctors' services that he could potentially get, from the competing doctors' fee schedules, "through" his health insurance company.

The health insurer would pool the buyers' payment to make the actual payment to the doctors for the insureds who become sick, but each buyer could take the income that he has allotted for health insurance and "spend" it by choosing the slate of healthcare services he would pay for at that price, selecting his doctor from among the competitors. Doctors would compete on the price to be chosen by each buyer when he decides how to allot his healthcare premium spend.

This would combine two novel approaches: "shopping" for treatment from the doctor, not the insurer, and expanding competition among health insurers by allowing small startup health insurers, akin to what was done for poor businesses in Asia by the "micro-credit" revolution that enabled any poor woman or man to open a business on a small loan. Thousands of small businesses will pop up to become micro-health insurers and facilitate the trade, between doctor and patient, of treatment for money.

This would connect the buyer to the seller and enable massive price competition among doctors, so costs would plummet, because many doctors would seek patients by offering cheaper prices at affordable levels of quality. Obviously this would not lower the quality of healthcare, because the doctors who succeeded would be those who proved they could deliver successful, effective treatments, but at cheaper prices. In today's world, where everyone finds ratings and reviews online, the doctors with the best value propositions, defined as higher quality at cheaper price, would be readily apparent.

The micro-health insurer could also prepay, locking the buyer and seller in at that price while taking profit up front and not when the healthcare is delivered. This would keep healthcare costs locked down at the competitive price the buyer chose to pay, and complete the sale for the buyer at the time of purchase, not after the fact when the patient-buyer becomes sick and his very life depends on paying for healthcare. Right now there are maybe a handful of insurers and 20 health insurance plans that compete in any given state Obamacare Exchange, but the initiative I have outlined would open the door to thousands of health insurers, and potentially hundreds of thousands of healthcare "menus" and "menu items" available to buyers pre-paying doctors a pro rata share of the healthcare premium cost of treatments received.

The analogy of healthcare options to a menu at a restaurant is a propos. People need food. If you don't have it, you die, just as a sick person who needs medical treatment gets it or dies. This does not enable the farms to jack up the price of food until it is out of sight, as doctors, hospitals, and pharmaceutical makers are doing. Instead, thousands of restaurants and grocery stores compete, buying food from farms and selling it as a selection of options on a menu.

People buy what they want, within the limits of their budget. Consumers win, and have tasty meals and full bellies. Yes, poor people may have to eat at cheap fast food stores, but they don't starve to death (and the food at Dunkin Donuts is not that bad!).

If you are willing to make do with less, such as by purchasing vegetables and cooking your food at home, you can eat quite nicely. So, too, could a free market system work for the benefit of all Americans by introducing price competition into the healthcare industry, which would create affordable options across a range of price points.

The conclusion to infer from this article is that, while the statists object that libertarian policy cannot be implemented in a practical manner, this is simply not true. Thinking outside the box, and being creative and innovative about policy solutions, will meet the challenge of making liberty work for America.

END.

------

[1] R.H. Coase, *The Problem of Social Cost*, 3 J.L. & Econ. 1-44 (1960).

[2] Guido Calabresi & A. Douglas Melamed, *Property Rules, Liability Rules, and Inalienability: One View of the Cathedral*, 85 Harv. L. Rev. 1089 (1972).

[3] R.H. Coase, *The Federal Communications Commission*, 2 J.L. & Econ 1-40 (1959).

ABOUT THE AUTHOR

Russell Hasan

Russell Hasan is the author of these books:

NONFICTION:

A System of Legal Logic: Using Aristotle, Ayn Rand, and Analytical Philosophy to Understand the Law, Interpret Cases, and Win in Litigation (A Scholarly Monograph)

If P Then Q: Why Philosophy Can Teach You How to Think and Help You Live a Happy Life By the Methods of Applying Logic to Solve the Problems in Your Life and Achieve Success (A Scholarly Monograph)

The Power of Objectivism: Ayn Rand and John Galt and Atlas Shrugged and The Morality of Life, Intelligence, Greed, Selfishness, Rationality, Individuality, Integrity, Capitalism, Desire, and Freedom

What They Won't Tell You About Objectivism: Thoughts on the Objectivist Philosophy in the Post-Randian Era

The Apple of Knowledge: Introducing the Philosophical Scientific Method and Pure Empirical Essential Reasoning

Golden Rule Libertarianism: A Defense of Freedom in Social, Economic, and Legal Policy

On Moral Psychology and Moral Philosophy: Towards a New Theory of Emotions, Motivations, and Ethics, Using the Insight that Emotions Pay Moral Debts and Moral Credits Owed to Self and Loved Ones (also published under the alternate first edition title On Forgiveness)

XYAB Economics: A GOLD Libertarian Analysis of Money, Trade, and Freedom

A Law and Economics Approach to Litigation Costs: The Proportionality Test for E-Discovery Law (A Scholarly Monograph)

FICTION:

The Paradise Machine

The Magic Key Cards

Fallen Angel and Other Contemporary Coming-of-Age Romance Short Stories

The Golden Wand Trilogy

Project Utopia: A Libertarian Science Fiction Anthology

The Office of Heavenly Restitution: A Fantasy Fiction Anthology

The Prince, The Girl and The Revolution: A Science Fiction Fairy Tale

Rob Seablue and The Eye of Tantalus

Russell Hasan (pronouns: He, him, his) is a graduate of Vassar College and graduated with Honors from the University of Connecticut School of Law. He is a proud member of the LGBTQIA+ community and an equally proud member of the Libertarian Party. Mr. Hasan has served as a member of the LGBTQ Rights Committee of the New York City Bar Association, and has been Vice Chair of the Libertarian Party Affiliate of Fairfield County, Connecticut. He loves coffee and chewing gum, and enjoys watching sports, comedies, and science fiction/fantasy tv shows and movies. His favorite books are Atlas Shrugged and The Fountainhead and his favorite movies are Star Wars and The Matrix.